TABLE OF CONTENT

Chapter 1: The Rich Dad's Mindset

Chapter 2: Lessons from the Rich Dad

Chapter 3: The Poor Dad's Mindset

Chapter 4: Pitfalls of the Poor Dad's Approach

Chapter 5: Breaking the Cycle: Transforming Mindsets

Chapter 6: Empowering Financial Literacy

Chapter 7: Summary

Copyright © 2024 by Olukayode Badejo

All rights reserved. No part of this book may be reproduced, distributed, or transmitted in any form or by any means, including photocopying, recording, or other electronic or mechanical methods, without the prior written permission of the publisher, except in the case of brief quotations embodied in critical reviews and certain other noncommercial uses permitted by copyright law.

For permission requests, write to the publisher, addressed "Attention: Permissions Coordinator," at the address below.

Lagos, Nigeria, 101233

kayus987@gmail.com

Introduction:

In the journey of life, our earliest influencers often leave an indelible mark on our perceptions, shaping the lens through which we view the world and its myriad opportunities. Among these influential figures are our parents, whose beliefs, attitudes, and actions towards wealth and financial prosperity can profoundly impact our own relationship with money.

In "Do You Have a Rich Dad or a Poor Dad?" we delve into the compelling concept of contrasting parental figures: the "rich dad" and the "poor dad." Drawing inspiration from various learning, we explore how the contrasting philosophies and behaviors of these parental archetypes mold a child's understanding of wealth and shape their financial destiny.

As we navigate through these pages, we embark on a journey of self-discovery, examining the lessons passed down from our caregivers and uncovering the hidden influences that continue to guide our financial decisions. Through insightful anecdotes, practical wisdom, and thought-provoking reflections, we uncover the pivotal role played by parental figures in instilling financial values and habits that can either propel us towards prosperity or hinder our path to financial freedom.

Indeed, the importance of understanding the lessons imparted by our parents regarding money management and wealth creation cannot be overstated. Whether we inherit the mindset of a "rich dad," characterized by entrepreneurship, strategic investing, and a mindset of abundance, or the perspective of a "poor dad," marked by scarcity, fear of risk, and reliance on conventional employment, our upbringing significantly shapes our financial trajectory.

In "Do You Have a Rich Dad or a Poor Dad?" we invite you to embark on a transformative journey of introspection and enlightenment. By exploring the contrasting influences of parental figures on our financial mindset, we empower ourselves to break free from limiting beliefs, embrace new possibilities, and chart a course towards true financial prosperity.

Join us as we unravel the mysteries of wealth, decode the lessons of our upbringing, and embark on a quest for financial empowerment and abundance. It's time to discover whether you have a rich dad or a poor dad—and, more importantly, to reclaim control of your financial destiny.

Chapter 1: The Rich Dad's Mindset

In the realm of wealth and prosperity, mindset reigns supreme. It is the lens through which we perceive opportunities, the foundation upon which we build our financial future, and the guiding force that shapes our decisions. In this chapter, we delve into the transformative mindset of the "rich dad," exploring the beliefs, values, and principles that distinguish their approach to money and wealth.

The Rich Dad's Approach to Money and Wealth

The rich dad sees money not as a scarce resource to be hoarded, but as a tool to be leveraged for greater abundance. Unlike the "poor dad," who views money through the lens of scarcity and limitation, the rich dad embraces a mindset of abundance and possibility. They understand that wealth is not finite but rather abundant, and that opportunities for financial growth abound for those who are willing to seek them out.

Financial Education as a Core Value

Central to the rich dad's mindset is the value of financial education. They recognize that traditional schooling often neglects to teach the fundamental principles of money management and wealth creation, leaving many individuals ill-prepared to navigate the complexities of the financial world. As such, the rich dad takes it upon themselves to impart crucial financial knowledge to their children, instilling in them the importance of understanding concepts such as budgeting, investing, and asset accumulation from an early age.

The Spirit of Entrepreneurship

Entrepreneurship is another cornerstone of the rich dad's mindset. They understand that true financial freedom lies not in reliance on a single source of income, but in the ability to create multiple streams of revenue through entrepreneurial endeavors. From starting small businesses to investing in income-generating assets, the rich dad encourages their children to cultivate an entrepreneurial spirit and pursue opportunities for wealth creation outside of traditional employment.

The Power of Investing

Investing is a key component of the rich dad's wealth-building strategy. They understand that by intelligently deploying their capital into assets that appreciate over time, they can exponentially grow their wealth and achieve long-term financial security. Whether it's investing in stocks, real estate, or business ventures, the rich dad teaches their children the value of strategic investing and the importance of making informed financial decisions.

Fostering Creativity and Risk-Taking

Central to the rich dad's mindset is the belief in the power of creativity and risk-taking. They understand that wealth is often generated through innovation and daring ventures, and they encourage their children to think outside the box, take calculated risks, and seize opportunities for wealth creation. By fostering a spirit of creativity and entrepreneurship, the rich dad empowers their children to overcome challenges, embrace failure as a learning opportunity, and ultimately achieve financial success.

Long-Term Wealth Preservation

Rather than living paycheck to paycheck or succumbing to lifestyle inflation, the Rich Dad prioritizes long-term wealth preservation. They practice frugality, live below their means, and allocate resources wisely to ensure financial stability and security for themselves and future generations.

Generosity and Philanthropy

Despite their focus on wealth accumulation, the Rich Dad understands the importance of giving back to society and making a positive impact in the world. They engage in philanthropic endeavors and use their wealth to support charitable causes and initiatives that align with their values.

Mindset of Abundance

The Rich Dad operates from a mindset of abundance rather than scarcity. They believe that opportunities are abundant and that there is enough wealth to go around for everyone. This mindset enables them to approach life with optimism, creativity, and a willingness to seize opportunities for financial growth and prosperity.

Generally, the rich dad's mindset is characterized by a belief in abundance, a commitment to financial education, a spirit of entrepreneurship, and a willingness to take calculated risks. By instilling these values in their children, the rich dad equips them with the tools and mindset necessary to navigate the complexities of the financial world and achieve lasting prosperity.

What did you learn from Chapter 1?

What steps will you start taking from now on?

....
....
....
....
....
....
....
....
....
....
....
....
....
....
....
....
....
....

Chapter 2: Lessons from the Rich Dad

In this chapter, we delve into the invaluable lessons imparted by a rich dad to their child about wealth accumulation and financial prosperity. Drawing from real-life experiences and practical wisdom, we explore the specific principles and strategies that guide the rich dad's approach to building and preserving wealth.

Lesson 1: Asset Acquisition

One of the fundamental principles taught by the rich dad is the importance of asset acquisition. Unlike liabilities, which drain financial resources, assets are vehicles for wealth accumulation and passive income generation. The rich dad instills in their child the value of acquiring income-producing assets such as real estate, stocks, and businesses, emphasizing the role of strategic investment in building long-term wealth.

For example, the rich dad may share their own experience of acquiring rental properties and generating steady rental income, highlighting the power of passive income to fuel financial growth and provide financial security for the future.

Lesson 2: Passive Income Generation

Passive income generation is another key lesson taught by the rich dad. They understand that relying solely on earned income from a job is limiting and unsustainable, and they encourage their child to diversify their income streams through passive income sources. Whether it's rental income from properties, dividends from stocks, or royalties from intellectual property, the rich dad emphasizes the importance of building multiple streams of passive income to achieve financial independence.

The rich dad may illustrate this lesson with anecdotes of how they established streams of passive income early in life, allowing them to enjoy financial freedom and pursue their passions without being tied to a traditional job.

Lesson 3: Wealth Preservation

Preserving wealth is a crucial aspect of the rich dad's teachings. They understand that accumulating wealth is only half the battle; it's equally important to safeguard it for future generations. The rich dad educates their child about the importance of prudent financial management, risk mitigation, and asset protection strategies to ensure the longevity of their wealth.

For instance, the rich dad may share stories of how they diversified their investment portfolio to mitigate risk, implemented tax-efficient strategies to minimize tax liabilities, and established estate plans to transfer wealth to heirs smoothly and efficiently.

Lesson 4: Philanthropy

Lastly, the rich dad instills in their child the value of giving back to society through philanthropy.

They understand that true wealth is not measured solely by financial abundance but by the impact we make on others and the world around us. The rich dad encourages their child to cultivate a spirit of generosity and compassion, using their wealth and resources to support charitable causes and make a positive difference in the lives of others.

The rich dad may recount personal anecdotes of how philanthropy has enriched their own life and brought fulfillment beyond financial success, inspiring their child to embrace a similar ethos of giving back.

Once upon a time, there lived a man named John who was a rich successful businessman. He had a son named James who was just 10 years old. John had always been a hardworking and determined individual, and he had built his wealth from scratch. He wanted his son to learn the value of hard work and have a rich mindset just like him.

John believed that a rich mindset was not just about having a lot of money, but also about having the right attitude towards life. He wanted James to understand the importance of financial literacy and how to make smart decisions with money.

To teach James about the rich mindset, John would often take him to his office and show him how his business operated. He would explain the concepts of investment, budgeting, and entrepreneurship in simple terms that James could understand.

John also encouraged James to read books about successfully rich entrepreneurs and their journeys to success. He wanted his son to learn from the experiences of others and gain a broader perspective on wealth and success.

One day, John took James to a charity event where they met a group of successful businessmen who had built their wealth by practising these principles. They shared their stories with James and talked about the importance of using one's wealth for the betterment of others. This left a lasting impression on James, and he realized that being rich was not just about accumulating wealth but also about making a positive impact on others.

John also taught James the value of hard work and perseverance. He made him work on small projects, such as setting up a lemonade stand, and taught him to save the profits for future investments. James learned that success does not come overnight, and it takes patience and dedication to achieve one's goals.

As James grew older, he started to show a keen interest in his father's business and started to help him with various tasks. John was proud to see his son's enthusiasm and encouraged him to pursue his dreams and passions.

Thanks to his father's teachings and guidance, James developed a rich mindset and went on to build a successful business worth over $50 million for himself. He used his wealth to support various charitable causes and inspired others to do the same.

John's influence on James was not just about teaching him how to make money, but it was about instilling values and principles that would guide him towards a fulfilling and successful life. James knew that he had a rich dad, not just in terms of money but also in terms of wisdom and guidance.

In conclusion, the lessons from the rich dad encompass asset acquisition, passive income generation, wealth preservation, and philanthropy. Through practical guidance, real-life examples, and personal anecdotes, the rich dad equips their child with the knowledge and mindset necessary to navigate the complexities of wealth accumulation and achieve lasting financial prosperity.

What did you learn from Chapter 2?

What steps will you start taking from now on?

....
....
....
....
....
....
....
....
....
....
....
....
....
....
....
....
....
....

Chapter 3: The Poor Dad's Mindset

In this chapter, we delve into the contrasting mindset of the "poor dad" towards money and wealth, exploring the beliefs, misconceptions, and limiting beliefs that perpetuate a cycle of financial struggle and scarcity.

The Poor Dad's Approach to Money and Wealth

Unlike the rich dad, who views money as a tool for abundance and prosperity, the poor dad approaches money with a mindset of fear and scarcity. They hold onto limiting beliefs about wealth, believing it to be elusive and unattainable, and often succumb to a cycle of financial struggle and instability.

Common Misconceptions and Limiting Beliefs

The poor dad's mindset is often shaped by common misconceptions and limiting beliefs about money and wealth. They may believe that wealth is reserved for the lucky few or that financial success is dependent on external factors beyond their control. These misconceptions create a sense of powerlessness and resignation, making it difficult for the poor dad to take proactive steps towards financial independence.

Furthermore, the poor dad may harbor deep-seated beliefs about money being inherently evil or corrupting, leading to a reluctance to pursue wealth and a fear of success. These limiting beliefs create a self-imposed barrier to financial growth and inhibit the poor dad from realizing their full potential.

The Influence of Fear-Based Mindset on Children

The fear-based mindset of the poor dad has a profound impact on their children's attitudes and behaviors towards money. Growing up in an environment characterized by financial struggle and scarcity, children of poor dads may internalize negative beliefs about money and develop unhealthy attitudes towards wealth.

For example, they may adopt a scarcity mindset, believing that there is never enough money to go around, or develop a fear of taking financial risks, fearing failure or loss. These attitudes and behaviors can perpetuate the cycle of poverty and inhibit the child's ability to break free from the limitations imposed by their upbringing.

In conclusion, the poor dad's mindset is characterized by fear, scarcity, and limiting beliefs about money and wealth. By exploring the misconceptions and influences that shape this mindset, we gain insight into the barriers to financial success and the challenges faced by individuals trapped in a cycle of financial struggle. Understanding the poor dad's mindset is the first step towards breaking free from its grip and creating a new path towards financial abundance and prosperity.

What did you learn from Chapter 3?

What steps will you start taking from now on?

Chapter 4: Pitfalls of the Poor Dad's Approach

In this chapter, we explore the detrimental consequences of adopting a poor dad's mindset and financial habits. We shed light on the risks associated with living paycheck to paycheck, accumulating debt, and relying solely on traditional employment for income. Additionally, we illustrate how a poor dad's mindset can lead to missed opportunities and hinder financial growth and prosperity.

The Perils of Living Paycheck to Paycheck

One of the most significant pitfalls of the poor dad's approach is the habit of living paycheck to paycheck. By spending all of their income as soon as it is received, without setting aside savings or investing for the future, individuals perpetuate a cycle of financial instability and vulnerability. They have no financial cushion to fall back on in case of emergencies or unexpected expenses, leaving them vulnerable to financial crises and setbacks.

Accumulating Debt and Financial Strain
Another consequence of the poor dad's mindset is the propensity to accumulate debt as a means of financing current lifestyle needs. Whether through credit cards, loans, or other forms of borrowing, individuals may find themselves trapped in a cycle of debt, struggling to keep up with interest payments and facing mounting financial strain. Debt can become a significant burden, draining financial resources and hindering long-term wealth accumulation.

Overreliance on Traditional Employment
Relying solely on traditional employment for income is another risk associated with the poor dad's approach. While steady employment provides a reliable source of income, it also limits financial growth and potential. Individuals who are content with a fixed salary may miss out on

opportunities to increase their earning potential through entrepreneurship, investments, or other alternative income streams. This narrow focus on earned income can hinder financial independence and limit opportunities for wealth creation.

Missed Opportunities and Hindered Financial Growth

Perhaps the most significant consequence of the poor dad's mindset is the missed opportunities for financial growth and prosperity. By clinging to limiting beliefs and outdated financial habits, individuals may fail to recognize or seize opportunities for wealth creation. Whether it's investing in assets, starting a business, or pursuing alternative income streams, the poor dad's mindset can blind individuals to the possibilities for financial success, leaving them trapped in a cycle of mediocrity and missed potential.

As a child, Jones always looked up to his father. He was a hardworking man, but no matter how much he worked, they could never seem to escape the clutches of poverty. Jones' father, Jack, always told him that money wasn't everything and that happiness came from within. However, as Jones grew older and saw his friends living in big houses and going on fancy vacations, he couldn't help but feel envious.

One day, Jones asked his father why they couldn't afford the same luxuries as his friends. Jack replied, "Because we don't need them. We have each other and that's all that matters." But deep down, Jack knew that he couldn't provide for his family the way he wanted to. He had a poor mindset, constantly telling himself that he wasn't meant to be rich and that it was better to be content with what they had.

As time went by, Jones started to adopt his father's poor mindset. He stopped dreaming big and settled for a mediocre job, just like his father. He believed that he was destined to be poor and there was nothing he could do about it. Jack's constant reminders that money wasn't everything and that they should be grateful for what they had only reinforced this belief in Jones' mind.

Even when opportunities presented themselves, Jones would shy away, thinking that he wasn't good enough or that he didn't deserve to be successful. He would often say things like, "Money corrupts people. I'd rather be poor and happy than rich and miserable." His poor mindset not only affected his career choices, but also his relationships. He pushed away anyone who had a different mindset, believing that they were only interested in his money.

As Jones grew older, he realized that his father's poor mindset had held him back from reaching his full potential. He saw his father struggling to make ends meet, and it dawned on him that he didn't want to end up like that. He started reading books about success and listening to motivational speakers, and slowly but surely, he began to change his mindset.

He learned that being rich didn't necessarily mean being greedy or unhappy. He saw that money could also be used for good and to help others. He started working hard, taking risks and grabbing opportunities that came his way. And soon enough, he became successful in his own right.

Looking back, Jones realized that his father's poor mindset had influenced him more than he had ever imagined. He wished his father had taught him the importance of financial literacy and the power of a rich mindset. But he also knew that his father had done the best he could with what he had. From that day on, Jones made a promise to himself to teach his own children the importance of having a rich mindset and the value of financial freedom.

In conclusion, adopting a poor dad's mindset and financial habits can have detrimental consequences, including living paycheck to paycheck, accumulating debt, over-reliance on traditional employment, and missed opportunities for financial growth. By understanding these pitfalls and the risks associated with the poor dad's approach, individuals can take proactive steps to break free from limiting beliefs, embrace new opportunities, and chart a course towards financial independence and prosperity.

What did you learn from Chapter 4?

....
....
....
....
....
....
....
....
....
....
....
....
....
....
....
....
....
....

What steps will you start taking from now on?

....
....
....
....
....
....
....
....
....
....
....
....
....
....
....
....
....
....

Chapter 5: Breaking the Cycle: Transforming Mindsets

In this chapter, we explore strategies and practical tips for breaking free from the limitations imposed by a poor dad's mindset. We delve into the importance of personal development, mindset shifts, and financial education in overcoming financial obstacles. Additionally, we share inspiring success stories of individuals who have transcended their upbringing to achieve financial abundance and prosperity.

Strategies for Breaking Free

Breaking free from the cycle of poverty requires intentional effort and a willingness to challenge ingrained beliefs and habits. One strategy is to cultivate a growth mindset, embracing the belief that our abilities and intelligence can be developed through dedication and hard work. By adopting a growth mindset, individuals can overcome self-limiting beliefs and embrace new opportunities for growth and success.

Another strategy is to invest in personal development and continuous learning. Whether through books, courses, or mentorship, individuals can expand their knowledge and skills, empowering themselves to take control of their financial future. Additionally, seeking out positive influences and surrounding oneself with like-minded individuals can provide invaluable support and encouragement on the journey towards financial independence.

Importance of Financial Education

Financial education is a cornerstone of breaking free from a poor dad's mindset. By gaining a solid understanding of basic financial principles such as budgeting, saving, investing, and debt management, individuals can make informed decisions about their money and take proactive steps towards financial security. Financial literacy empowers individuals to build wealth, achieve financial goals, and create a better future for themselves and their families.

Mindset Shifts for Success

Shifting from a scarcity mindset to an abundance mindset is essential for transcending the limitations imposed by a poor dad's mindset. By focusing on opportunities rather than obstacles, cultivating gratitude, and embracing a positive outlook, individuals can attract abundance into their lives and manifest their financial goals. Additionally, adopting a mindset of resilience and perseverance enables individuals to overcome setbacks and stay committed to their financial journey, even in the face of adversity.

Inspiring Success Stories

Throughout history, countless individuals have risen above their circumstances to achieve financial abundance and prosperity. From rags to riches stories of self-made entrepreneurs to tales of perseverance and resilience in the face of adversity, these success stories serve as inspiration for those seeking to break free from the cycle of poverty. By studying the journeys of successful individuals and learning from their experiences, individuals can glean valuable insights and strategies for overcoming financial obstacles and achieving their own version of success.

In conclusion, breaking free from a poor dad's mindset requires a combination of strategies, including personal development, financial education, and mindset shifts. By embracing growth, learning, and resilience, individuals can transcend their upbringing and create a life of financial abundance and prosperity. With determination and perseverance, anyone can rewrite their financial story and build a brighter future for themselves and generations to come.

What did you learn from Chapter 5?

What steps will you start taking from now on?

Chapter 6: Empowering Financial Literacy

In this chapter, we advocate for the importance of financial literacy and education in empowering individuals to take control of their financial destiny. We offer resources and recommendations for learning about personal finance, investing, and wealth building. Additionally, we encourage readers to embrace lifelong learning and adopt the mindset of a rich dad to create a legacy of financial prosperity for future generations.

The Power of Financial Literacy

Financial literacy is the cornerstone of financial empowerment. By understanding basic financial concepts and principles, individuals can make informed decisions about their money, plan for the future, and build wealth over time. Financial literacy equips individuals with the knowledge and skills they need to navigate the complexities of the financial world and achieve their financial goals.

Resources for Learning

Fortunately, there are numerous resources available to help individuals enhance their financial literacy and education. From books and online courses to podcasts and seminars, there are endless opportunities for learning about personal finance, investing, and wealth building. Some recommended resources include:

Books:

- Rich Dad Poor Dad" by Robert Kiyosaki
- The Millionaire Next Door by Thomas J. Stanley and William D. Danko
- The Intelligent Investor by Benjamin Graham
- The Science of Getting Rich by Wallace D. Wattles

Podcasts:
- The Dave Ramsey Show
- The BiggerPockets Podcast
- Afford Anything

Seminars and Workshops:
Financial literacy workshops offered by local community organizations, investment seminars hosted by financial professionals.

Embracing Lifelong Learning

Financial literacy is not a destination but a journey. It's important for individuals to embrace lifelong learning and continually seek out opportunities to expand their knowledge and skills. By staying curious, open-minded, and committed to personal growth, individuals can stay ahead of the curve and adapt to changes in the financial landscape.

Adopting the Mindset of a Rich Dad

Finally, we encourage readers to adopt the mindset of a rich dad and strive for financial independence and prosperity. This mindset is characterized by a focus on asset acquisition, passive income generation, wealth preservation, and philanthropy. By thinking like a rich dad and taking proactive steps towards financial success, individuals can create a legacy of wealth and abundance that extends far beyond their own lifetime.

In conclusion, empowering financial literacy is essential for individuals to take control of their financial destiny and build a brighter future for themselves and their families. By accessing resources, embracing lifelong learning, and adopting the mindset of a rich dad, anyone can achieve financial independence and create a legacy of prosperity for generations to come.

What did you learn from Chapter 6?

What steps will you start taking from now on?

....
....
....
....
....
....
....
....
....
....
....
....
....
....
....
....
....
....
....

Chapter 7: Summary

In conclusion, "Do You Have a Rich Dad or a Poor Dad?" offers valuable insights gained from contrasting the perspectives of a rich dad versus a poor dad. Through exploring the mindset, beliefs, and financial habits of each, readers gain a deeper understanding of the factors that influence their own relationship with money.

Key lessons include recognizing the importance of mindset in shaping financial outcomes, understanding the impact of upbringing on financial beliefs and behaviors, and embracing financial literacy as a tool for empowerment. By contrasting the values of financial education, entrepreneurship, and investing instilled by a rich dad with the fear-based mindset and limiting beliefs perpetuated by a poor dad, readers are encouraged to reflect on their own upbringing and beliefs about money.

Empowered with this knowledge, readers are encouraged to take actionable steps towards achieving financial freedom and prosperity. This may include investing in personal development, seeking out financial education resources, and adopting the mindset of a rich dad to create a legacy of wealth and abundance. Regardless of one's background or upbringing, it is never too late to rewrite the narrative and create a wealthy legacy for oneself and future generations.

In essence, "Do You Have a Rich Dad or a Poor Dad?" serves as a guide for readers to transcend the limitations imposed by their upbringing, embrace financial empowerment, and chart a course towards a brighter financial future. By taking ownership of their financial destiny and embracing the principles of wealth creation, readers can transform their lives and create a legacy of prosperity for generations to come.

www.ingramcontent.com/pod-product-compliance
Lightning Source LLC
Chambersburg PA
CBHW070946220526
45471CB00007B/2916